New Vanguard • 84

OSPREY
PUBLISHING

German Light Cruisers 1939–45

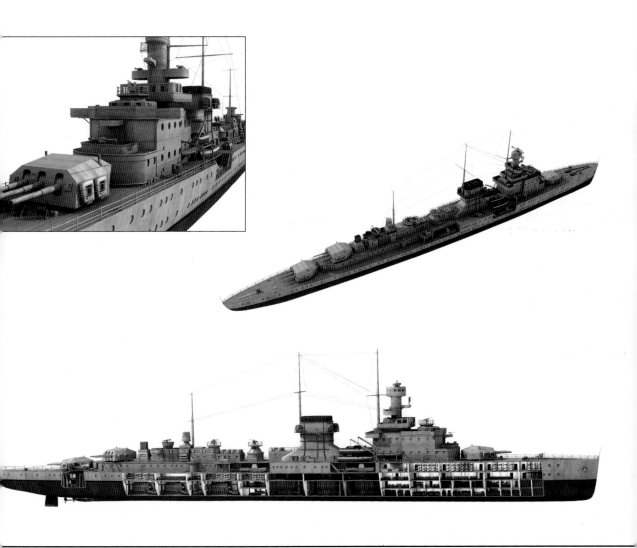

Gordon Williamson • Illustrated by Ian Palmer

First published in Great Britain in 2003 by Osprey Publishing, Elms Court, Chapel Way, Botley, Oxford OX2 9LP, United Kingdom.
Email: info@ospreypublishing.com

ISBN 1 84176 503 1

Editor: Simone Drinkwater
Design: Melissa Orrom Swan
Index by Bob Munro

Originated by Grasmere Digital Imaging, Leeds, UK
Printed in China through World Print Ltd.

03 04 05 06   10 9 8 7 6 5 4 3 2 1

A CIP catalogue record for this book is available from the British Library

For a catalogue of all books published by Osprey Military and Aviation please contact:

Osprey Direct UK, P.O. Box 140, Wellingborough, Northants, NN8 2FA, UK
E-mail: info@ospreydirect.co.uk

Osprey Direct USA, c/o MBI Publishing, P.O. Box 1, 729 Prospect Ave, Osceola, WI 54020, USA
E-mail: info@ospreydirectusa.com

www.ospreypublishing.com

Author's note

Unless otherwise specified, the photographs used in this work were provided by the *U-Boot Archiv* in Cuxhaven-Altenbruch and I would like to express my gratitude to the Director of the *Archiv*, Horst Bredow, for his permission to reproduce these photos. Whilst the *U-Boot Archiv* might to some seem an unlikely source of photos of surface ships, it should be remembered that many U-boat men were former crewmembers of surface vessels and many of their personal photos have been donated to the *Archiv*. The *Archiv* also benefited from the donation of a huge number of photographic negatives from a former war correspondent, Walter Schöppe, including many photos of surface ships.

Artist's note

Readers may care to note that the original paintings from which the colour plates in this book were prepared are available for private sale. All reproduction copyright whatsoever is retained by the Publishers. All enquiries should be addressed to:

Ian Palmer, 15 Floriston Avenue, Hillingdon, Middlesex, UB10 9DZ, UK

The Publishers regret that they can enter into no correspondence upon this matter.

GERMAN LIGHT CRUISERS 1939–45

INTRODUCTION

In April 1919, the German government passed legislation governing the creation of a new navy, titled the Reichsmarine, replacing the Imperial German Navy of the Kaiser's era. The High Seas Fleet had been ordered by the Allies to sail into the British base at Scapa Flow and there, after hearing the final terms of the Treaty of Versailles on 21 June, the German commanders had been ordered by Admiral Reuter to scuttle their vessels to prevent their subsequent use by the Allies. Enraged by the scuttling of the Fleet at Scapa Flow, the Allies simply seized most of the remaining German ships in reprisal, thus reducing the once powerful German fleet, boasting some of the most modern and powerful warships in existence, to a motley collection of light cruisers and obsolete pre-dreadnoughts.

The Treaty of Versailles, signed by Germany on 28 June 1919, severely restricted the size and number of warships Germany was permitted.

Germany was restricted to six old pre-dreadnought battleships, six light cruisers, 12 destroyers and 12 torpedo boats. No submarines were permitted. Naval manpower was to be kept to a total of 15,000, of which only 1,500 were to be of officer rank. The Armed Forces Law, passed by the Reichstag on 21 March 1921, stipulated that a further two pre-dreadnought battleships and two light cruisers could be held in reserve.

The terms of the Treaty of Versailles stated that these ships could not be replaced, let alone added to, until they were at least 20 years old. By 1923, however, only two battleships, the *Hannover* and *Braunschweig*, were in service, together with five cruisers and a number of torpedo boats. Thus, faced with restraints on manpower and in warship construction, as

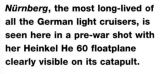

Nürnberg, the most long-lived of all the German light cruisers, is seen here in a pre-war shot with her Heinkel He 60 floatplane clearly visible on its catapult.

well as a devastating economic burden of crippling reparation payments to her former enemies, the outlook for the German navy was bleak. Germany had lost her best and most modern warships but was now in the position of being able to rebuild her fleet with new vessels, whilst making use of the most up-to-date technology. Thus, although small in size, the Reichsmarine would possess some of the world's most modern warships at the beginning of World War Two.

By 1925, the K class of modern light cruisers (the *Königsberg*, *Köln* and *Karlsruhe*) had been added to the fleet, joined in 1927 by the *Leipzig*.

The terms of the Washington Agreement of February 1922 had laid restrictions on warship construction in an attempt to prevent an arms race. Although all of the major powers had signed, Germany had not been invited to attend. It was clear, however, that she would be held to the same terms. The Agreement classified ships into two categories: capital ships with guns greater than 20cm calibre, and smaller ships with guns of a lesser calibre and with a maximum displacement of 11,900 metric tons (10,000 Imperial tons). This latter category was one that the Germans saw as providing them with a great opportunity to create new and relatively powerful warships.

View forward from the bridge of a K-class cruiser. The narrow beam of this class is evident. Note the forward 6m rangefinder in view at the bottom.

A further treaty, the London Naval Agreement of April 1930, divided the cruiser class into two types, the heavy cruiser and the light cruiser. As both types were to be restricted to the 10,000-ton limit already mentioned, the classification clearly referred to the armament rather than the displacement of these vessels. The light cruiser would be permitted main armament of up to 15.5cm calibre (6.1in.) and the heavy cruiser up to 20.3cm (8in.). Existing laws, however, still set the maximum level of cruiser strength of the Reichsmarine at six light cruisers, no provision being made for the heavier type.

It was not until the conclusion of the Anglo-German Naval Treaty of June 1935 that such restrictions were set aside, the new restrictions simply setting the German Navy's total strength at 35 per cent of that of the Royal Navy, but no longer with any restriction of the numbers on individual warship types. The terms effectively left Germany able to plan for the construction of five heavy cruisers, totalling just over 50,000 tons, within the terms of the London Naval Agreement.

THE LIGHT CRUISER

Firepower

The 15cm gun mounted in triple gun turrets was the standard armament on the majority of German light cruisers. In German terminology, turrets were identified by letters, from bow to stern, thus 'Anton', 'Bruno',

'Caesar' and 'Dora'. The majority of the light cruisers carried only one forward turret, 'Anton', and two at the stern, 'Bruno' and 'Caesar'.

The 15cm gun had a muzzle velocity of 960mps and fired a 45.5kg shell for a maximum range, depending on trajectory, of up to 25,700m. Each barrel, including its breech mechanism, weighed just under 12 tons. There were three different types of projectile for these weapons: an armour-piercing shot, containing 0.9kg of TNT, and two high explosive types, one with a 3.9kg TNT charge and the other with a smaller 3kg charge. Barrel life was estimated at around 500 rounds, after which it would need to be replaced.

Here we see gun crews manning the two single-barrelled 8.8cm flak guns on one of the K-class cruisers. The lengthy script on the sailors' cap tally ribbons suggest the vessel is *Königsberg* or *Karlsruhe*.

The 8.8cm flak gun

The 8.8cm flak gun used aboard the light cruisers came in two forms: the L/45 in a single-barrelled mount, and the L/76 in a twin mount. The former had a muzzle velocity of 790mps, whilst the later twin mount had a muzzle velocity of 950mps. These weapons fired a 9kg shell to a range of up to 17,200m.

The 10.5cm flak gun

The 10.5cm twin flak mounts on the light cruisers were of the same type installed on their heavy counterparts and featured triaxially stabilised carriages. They fired with a muzzle velocity of 900mps, discharging a 15.1kg projectile for a range of up to 17,700m against surface targets and 12,500m against aerial targets. Barrel life was around 2,950 rounds and somewhere in the region of 6,500 rounds of 10.5cm ammunition was carried, including in the region of 240 rounds of tracer.

The 3.7cm flak gun

The secondary flak armament on the light cruisers, as on most of the larger German warships, was the 3.7cm twin flak gun. This weapon fired a 0.74kg projectile at a muzzle velocity of 1,000mps and had a range of around 8,500m against surface targets and 6,800m against aerial targets. Barrel life was around 7,500 rounds. Practical rate of fire was around 80 rounds per minute though as much as double this was possible in theory. The total number of 3.7cm guns carried could and did vary during wartime, and around 4,000 rounds of ammunition per barrel were carried.

The 2cm flak gun

This prolifically produced weapon was installed on all types of vessel, from U-boats to battleships. They were used in single, twin and quadruple configuration. The 2cm flak gun fired a 39.5g projectile with a muzzle velocity of 835mps with a range from 4,900m against surface targets to 3,700m against aerial targets. A maximum rate of fire of up to 280 rounds per minute per barrel was theoretically possible, but a rate of around 120 rounds per minute was usual. This meant that the four-barrelled *Flakvierling* would fire at least 480 rounds per minute and usually nearer to 800, and with several such weapons in place a substantial hail of fire could be put up against low-flying aircraft that came too close. Approximately 3,000 rounds of 2cm ammunition were carried for each barrel.

Towards the end of the war, flak armament on most German warships was considerably enhanced. In addition, a limited number of 4cm Bofors flak guns were also installed on German vessels (again ranging from small E-boats up to capital ships) in the latter stages of the war. These fired a 0.96kg projectile with a muzzle velocity of 854mps and had a range of up to 7,000m.

View down into the bridge area of a K-class cruiser. Note the 'flying bridge' extension walkways. On some larger ships these could be swung inboard, but on these cruisers they were fixed structures.

Torpedoes

The light cruisers each carried four triple-torpedo-tube rotating mounts, two to port and two to starboard. Initially, the light cruisers carried 50cm tubes but these were subsequently changed to the superior 53cm type. The torpedoes carried were the G7a type, weighing just over 1.5 tons. They were capable of speeds up to 44 knots. Twelve torpedoes were carried loaded in the tubes, with a further 12 stored. Through the course of the war several of the cruisers had their complement of torpedo tubes either reduced or completely removed.

Radar

The German navy played a leading role in the development of military radar systems. The Nachrichten Versuchsabteilung (NSV) had begun work on the development of sonar-type systems capable of detecting underwater targets as early as 1929. Using similar principles for operating above the surface, a rather primitive system was developed

On this shot taken from the stern of *Köln*, the off-centre placement of turrets 'Bruno' and 'Caesar' is clear. This allowed them to traverse towards the bow further than would have been possible on a centre-line placement. It was not a particularly significant aid to the ship's effectiveness and was not continued beyond the K class.

in 1933 that could pick up echoes using 13.5cm short-wave transmissions. In 1934 a new organisation, the Gesellschaft für Elektroakustische und Mechanische Apparate (GEMA) was founded to continue development in this area. The two organisations now strove to outdo each other in the attempt to produce an effective radio detection apparatus. By September 1935 a 48cm wavelength (630 MHz) set was tested before the CinC Navy, Admiral Raeder, and produced positive results using the training ship *Bremse* as a target (admittedly a rather large one).

The set was then installed for a time on the *Welle*, this small and rather unimposing vessel becoming the first German navy ship to carry functioning radar equipment. The set was tweaked somewhat to improve efficiency, settling on a wavelength of 82cm (368MHz), which became the standard for all naval radar sets. German naval radar sets produced during this period and through to 1945 were predominantly developed by GEMA along with well-known firms such as Telefunken, Siemens, Lorenz and AEG.

German naval radar used a bewildering range of designations. In some cases this was deliberate and intended to confuse enemy intelligence. Early sets, for example, were referred to as DeTe (Dezimeter-Telegraphie) in an effort to disguise the true intent of the equipment.

Early operational radar sets were referred to as FMG (Funkmess-Gerät) or radar equipment, with suffixes indicating the year of manufacture, manufacturing company, frequency code letter and location on board ship. Thus, the set FMG 39G (gO), first installed on the *Admiral Graf Spee*, indicated: FMG – Fumkmess-Gerät; 39 – 1939; G – GEMA; g – code for 335 to 430 MHz and O indicating its position as being mounted on the foretop rangefinder.

To confuse matters further, as radar developed, even more classification terminology was introduced, including names as well as numbers. The FuSE 80 *Freya*, for instance, indicated: Fu – Funkmess or radar; S – Siemens, the manufacturer; E – Erkennung, search or reconnaissance radar; 80 – the development number; and *Freya* – the code name.

Fortunately, in 1943, a new, simplified designation system was introduced, in which the sets employed by the navy bore the designations FuMO (Funkmess-Ortung) active search radar, or FuMB (Funkmess-Beobachtung) passive detecting radar. This was then followed by a specific numerical code. Not all of the light cruisers were fitted with radar, but for those which were, the predominant types used were the FuMO 21, FuMO 24/25, FuMO 63, FuMB 6 and FuMB 4.

Fire control
Turret 'Anton'
The forward main turret of each ship was controlled by a 6m optical rangefinder unit mounted in an electrically-powered rotating housing on the ship's foretop. In addition, a further 6m rangefinder was positioned in the forward fire control centre on the forward main superstructure just aft of turret 'Anton'.

Turrets 'Bruno' and 'Caesar'
The aft main turrets could be controlled by the foretop rangefinder or the 6m rangefinder mounted on the aft main fire control position.

Flak
Main fire control for the heavy 8.8cm or 10.5cm twin flak guns was provided by three 3m rangefinders, one either side of the bridge and one mounted on the after fire control centre. These fed data down to battle control positions below decks.

Aircraft
The K-class cruisers were fitted with aircraft catapults in 1935. The standard shipboard aircraft on German warships prior to the outbreak of war was the two-seater Heinkel He 60 biplane. This aircraft was intended for a scouting and reconnaissance role and was armed with only a single machine gun. It was normal for two to be carried, one on the catapult, and another disassembled in storage. (There were no aircraft hangars on the light cruisers.) This aircraft was replaced as the standard shipboard aircraft for the Kriegsmarine prior to the outbreak of World War Two by the superior Arado Ar 196. This two-seater monoplane carried cannon as well as machine gun armament and could also carry 50kg bombs.

Ships' names
Unlike so many German warships in World War Two, which were named after historical characters, the light cruisers were all named for German cities. In each case the heraldic crest, carried originally on the bows of these vessels, was therefore that of the city whose name it bore. Emden also wore on her stem a large black Iron Cross motif carried in honour of the part her predecessor played in the Battle of the Falkland Islands in 1914.

Turrets 'Bruno' and 'Caesar' on the *Nürnberg*. Note that these turrets have reverted to a more conventional centre-line placement. Also of interest is the crest on turret 'Caesar'. This is the family crest of Maximilian Graf von Spee, and was carried in remembrance of Graf Spee's historic encounter with a British cruiser force off the Falklands in 1914. Each of *Nürnberg*'s main armament turrets carried a commemorative crest.

KREUZER EMDEN

EMDEN SPECIFICATIONS

Length	155.1m
Beam	14.3m
Draught	5.93m
Maximum displacement	6,990 tons
Maximum speed	29.5 knots
Maximum endurance	5,300 nautical miles
Main armament	8 x 15cm guns in eight single gun turrets
Secondary armament	3 x 8.8cm guns in single mounts (later 3 x 10.5cm twin barrel mounts)
Flak Armament	4 x 3.7cm guns on single mounts
	7 x 2cm guns on single mounts
	2 x 2cm *Flakvierling*
Torpedoes	4 x 50cm torpedo tubes in two twin mounts
Aircraft	None
Complement	19 officers and 464 men

Ship's commanders

Kapitän zur See Foerster	Oct 1925–Dec 1928
Fregattenkapitän Lothar Arnauld de la Periere	Dec 1928–Oct 1930
Fregattenkapitän Witthoeft-Emden	Oct 1930–Mar 1932
Fregattenkapitän Grassmann	Mar 1932–Sep 1934
Fregattenkapitän Karl Dönitz	Sep 1934–Sep 1935
Fregattenkapitän Bachmann	Sep 1935–Aug 1936
Kapitän zur See Lohmann	Aug 1936–Jul 1937
Fregattenkapitän Bürkner	Jul 1937–Jun 1938
Kapitän zur See Wever	Jun 1938–May 1939
Kapitän zur See Werner Lange	May 1939–Aug 1940
Kapitän zur See Mirow	Aug 1940–Jul 1942
Kapitän zur See Friedrich Traugott Schmidt	Jul 1942–Sep 1943
Kapitän zur See Henigst	Sep 1943–Mar 1944
Fregattenkapitän Hans-Eberhard Meissner	Mar 1944–Jan 1945
Kapitän zur See Wolfgang Kähler	Jan 1945–May 1945

General construction data

Emden was the sole example of her class, her design severely restricted by conditions imposed by the Allied Control Commission, and was based on the design concept for the Imperial Navy cruiser *Karlsruhe*. The original intent to have the armament in the conventional layout of four turrets, each with two gun barrels, was overruled by the Allies who insisted on eight single-barrelled turrets. Four were placed in the traditional layout, on the ship's centre line, two forward and two aft. One turret was placed either side of the main forward super-structure and one either side of the aft superstructure to the rear of the aftermost funnel. This layout meant that only six guns of the ship's main armament could be brought to bear in a broadside rather than the full eight.

Emden was protected by an armoured deck ranging in thickness from 20mm to 40mm and by a 50mm armour belt on her hull. Her armoured control tower was protected by 100mm of armour.

The *Emden* was the first modern light cruiser to be constructed for the German navy after World War One. The contract for her construction was placed with the Marinewerft in Wilhelmshaven on 7 April 1921 and the keel laid some eight months later. Construction took just over four years and she was launched on 7 January 1925. After fitting out and finishing work was completed, *Emden* was commissioned into the Reichsmarine on 15 October 1925.

Modifications

Modifications seem to have been made to *Emden* almost constantly over her career. Those that follow relate only to instances when a number of significant modifications were made at the same time.

Emden's first modifications were carried out over the winter of 1925–26 and consisted of a shortening of her battlemast by some seven metres (23ft) and a remodelling of her foretop. At the same time, the aft funnel, originally shorter than the forward funnel, was heightened. A flying bridge was also constructed at the base of the battlemast.

In April 1933, *Emden*'s original coal-fired boilers were replaced by more modern oil-fired units.

The next major modifications came in 1934, when both funnels were reduced by some two metres (6½ft) in height. The mainmast was greatly reduced in height, so as to be tall enough to accommodate the searchlight platforms it carried. Aerial masts were attached to the rear funnel and a small crane installed to the starboard side of the mainmast.

Further modifications carried out in 1936 saw a pole mast attached to the rear of the shortened mainmast, a single aerial mast attached to the rear face of the aft funnel to replace the various smaller antennae, and a third 8.8cm flak gun added.

Following the outbreak of war, in September 1939 a degaussing coil to protect against magnetic mines was added around her hull side just above the waterline. Finally, in 1942, the lower platform on her battlemast had its searchlights removed and was modified to take a FuMB

Immediately identifiable by the combination of the single funnel and placement of the aircraft catapult astern rather than in front of the funnel, this is *Nürnberg* recovering her Heinkel He 60 floatplane. Note that pre-war, these aircraft were in a plain pale grey livery and carried a large swastika banner insignia on the tailplane.

Emden pulls into port with her crew mustered on deck. At this time she still has the tall mainmast.

Emden returning from one of her world cruises. Many of Germany's future top naval commanders undertook such cruises as cadets on this ship. A warm welcome always awaited *Emden* on her return from these flag-waving cruises.

radar antenna. Between 1942 and 1943 some enhancement was made to *Emden*'s flak gun complement, with 2cm *Flakvierling* installed abaft the midships main armament turrets. Two additional 2cm single-barrelled flak guns were added to the navigating bridge platform and two 4cm guns on the bridge deck.

Powerplant

Emden was driven by two propeller shafts, each with a three-bladed propeller. Power was provided by Braun-Boverie turbines, one high-pressure and one low-pressure unit coupled to each shaft. The turbines were fed by a total of ten boilers, six of which were oil-fired and four of which were older coal-fired types. These coal-fired units were removed during refit in 1933 so that thereafter all of her boilers were the more modern oil-fired type. For auxiliary power, three 420kW diesel generators were provided. *Emden* was steered with a single rudder.

Service

Emden's primary role prior to the outbreak of World War Two was as a training ship. One glance at the list of her commanders during this period reveals the names of many who went on to have distinguished careers, including the final CinC Navy, Grossadmiral Karl Dönitz.

Though modest in armour and armament, and based on outdated design concepts, *Emden* served the navy well, showing the flag on several world cruises. There was virtually no part of the world that this cruiser did not visit and the world cruise with *Emden* was to be an essential part of the training of many officer cadets.

On the outbreak of war, *Emden* took part in defensive minelaying operations off the German coast. The war came to her early, however, as on completing her first trip and returning for a second load of mines she was caught up in a British air raid on Wilhelmshaven. As she lay at the quayside, *Emden* came under attack. Defensive anti-aircraft fire took out one of the attackers, but unfortunately the doomed aircraft crashed into the cruiser and 29 crew were killed or injured.

Emden's next sortie was another which ended in disaster, though not for her. The cruiser sailed from Swinemünde along with *Lützow*, *Blücher*

and a number of smaller escorts during Operation Weserübung, the invasion of Norway. Their target was the port of Oslo. The German ships were entering Oslofjord when the lead ship, *Blücher*, was illuminated by Norwegian searchlights, came under heavy fire from shore batteries and was mortally wounded, eventually capsizing with considerable loss of life. Unable to proceed further up the fjord beyond this point, *Lützow* and *Emden* disembarked the troops they were carrying further down the fjord, for an assault over land on the Norwegian fortifications at Dröbak, whilst the two ships would provide covering fire for the assault. In the event, the Norwegians surrendered without offering any resistance. Once resistance in the area ended, *Emden* moved up the fjord to Oslo where she served as an inter-services communications centre. Thereafter, the cruiser was allocated to training duties, a task she fulfilled until September 1941.

Following on the invasion of the Soviet Union in the summer of 1941, *Emden* was allocated to the port of Libau on the Baltic along with the light cruiser *Leipzig*, and in late September took part in fire support missions to aid German troops assaulting the Soviet-held Estonian island of Ösel. Only a few weeks later, however, she was re-assigned once again to training duties, on which she served until June 1942 when she returned to Wilhelmshaven for overhaul and refit.

On completion of repairs and improvements, *Emden* returned to her training duties in the Baltic, attending to these tasks until 1944. In September of that year, she returned to Norwegian waters once again and was allocated to the CinC Minelayers as his flagship. She took part in numerous minelaying operations in September and October before being tasked with running escort missions for troop convoys in and out of Oslo.

In December the veteran cruiser ran aground in Oslofjord near the island of Flateguri and required dockyard repairs. She was sent to Königsberg where, before her repairs at the Schichau yard were completed, she took on board the mortal remains of Generalfeld-marschall Hindenburg and his wife, which had been disinterred to prevent them falling into the hands of the approaching Soviets who by this time were only around 40km (25 miles) or so to the east, and was towed to Pillau. Here the remains of the field marshal and his wife were removed and *Emden*'s engines put into running order, though still not capable of making best speed. Her guns, which had also been removed,

This post-refit photograph clearly shows the increase in height of the second funnel, the addition of a pole mast to the rear face of that funnel, and reduction of the mainmast to little more than a stump to accommodate the searchlight platforms.

were re-installed at the same time. Now at least *Emden* could once again be considered a warship, albeit not fully effective.

Emden then loaded up with refugees fleeing from the advancing Red Army, and sailed for Kiel on 1 February 1945. Having disembarked her passengers, she was taken into the Deutsche Werke yard on 7 February for completion of outstanding repairs. Whilst in dry dock she was severely damaged on two separate occasions by British bombers. Eventually, on 14 April, listing badly, she was towed to Heikendorfer Bay where she was grounded. On 3 May explosive charges were set and she was blown up to prevent her falling into enemy hands.

THE K-CLASS CRUISERS

This class of cruiser, of which three, the *Königsberg*, *Köln* and *Karlsruhe* were built, was classed as *Spähkreuzer*, literally reconnaissance or scouting cruiser. They were never intended to give serious battle to equivalent enemy warships, but rather to 'hit and run'. Thus, six of their nine 15cm guns were mounted in two triple turrets facing aft, to give her a better chance of fending off pursuing enemy ships. In the K class, the two aft turrets were also mounted off centre, allowing these stern turrets to traverse further round in the direction of the bow and be brought into action if the cruiser was pursuing a victim.

The severe treaty restrictions under whose terms the K-class cruisers were built, and the many weight-saving measures employed, resulted in vessels that were rather weak structurally, as would be proven by the storm damage suffered by *Karlsruhe* during her 1936 cruise to the Pacific. In addition, the effective range without refuelling was rather modest when compared with ships such as the pocket battleships and heavy cruisers that were built later. The K class were not really suitable for long-distance operational use, indeed being inferior to the older *Emden* in this respect, and in the event, after the outbreak of war, they were restricted to coastal duties.

Powerplant
The K-class cruisers were driven by two propeller shafts, each with a three-bladed propeller. To each shaft were coupled a high-pressure and a low-pressure turbine, which were capable of being operated either together or independently, plus a diesel engine that could be used for more fuel-economic cruising. The ship's turbines were fed by six oil-fired boilers. The diesel engines were sited in the aftermost compartment of

A superb broadside shot of *Königsberg* after her 1935 refit and the addition of an aircraft catapult forward of the first funnel. Note also the individual single-barrelled 8.8cm flak guns forward of turret 'Bruno' have been replaced by a more modern twin unit.

the engine room, followed by the low-pressure turbines and the high-pressure turbines. Forward of the high-pressure turbine compartment lay the first boiler room compartment with one pair of boilers, one to port and one to starboard, followed by a similarly equipped compartment. The next two compartments featured one boiler each, mounted on the ship's centre line. The ship was steered by means of a single rudder.

Radar

Neither *Königsberg* nor *Karlsruhe* were fitted with radar. *Köln*, however, had a FuMO 21 radar set installed in place of the forward 6m rangefinder.

KREUZER KÖNIGSBERG

KÖNIGSBERG SPECIFICATIONS	
Length	169m
Beam	15.2m
Draught	5.7m
Maximum displacement	6.750 tons
Maximum speed	32 knots
Maximum endurance	5,700 nautical miles (turbines)
	8,000 nautical miles (diesels)
Main armament	9 x 15cm guns in three triple gun turrets
Secondary armament	12 x 10.5cm guns in six twin turrets
Flak armament	12 x 3.7cm guns in six twin turrets
	8 x 2cm guns on single mounts
Torpedoes	12 x 53.3cm torpedo tubes in four triple mounts
Aircraft	2 x Heinkel He 60 floatplanes
Complement	50 officers and 1,500 men

Ship's commanders

Kapitän zur See Wolf von Trotha	Apr 1929–Jun 1929
Fregattenkapitän Robert Witthöft-Emden	Jun 1929–Sep 1930
Fregattenkapitän Hermann Densch	Sep 1930–Sep 1931
Fregattenkapitän Otto von Schrader	Sep 1931–Sep 1934
Fregattenkapitän Hubert Schmundt	Sep 1934–Sep 1935
Fregattenkapitän Bachmann	Sep 1935–Feb 1937
Fregattenkapitän Robin Schall-Emden	Feb 1937–Nov 1938
Kapitän zur See Ernst Scheurlen	Nov 1938–Jun 1939
Kapitän zur See Kurt-Caesar Hoffmann	Jun 1939–Sep 1939
Kapitän zur See Heinrich Ruhfus	Sep 1939–May 1940

General construction data

Königsberg was the first of the three K-class cruisers to be laid down. The original order for her construction was issued to the Marinewerft in Wilhelmshaven in 1925 and her keel was laid in April 1926. Basic construction took just under a year, the cruiser being launched in April 1929. Exactly eight months later, in December 1929, with her fitting out work completed, she was commissioned into the Reichsmarine. *Königsberg* was allocated as flagship of the newly created Aufklärungs streitekräfte, or reconnaissance forces, and took part in a series of goodwill cruises showing the flag in various Mediterranean ports.

A bow view of *Königsberg* showing to good effect her heraldic crest, mounted on the stem itself. This was later deleted and a shield fitted either side of the bow. The forward and foretop 6m rangefinders are also seen to good advantage.

Modifications

Königsberg received her first major modifications in 1931 when the mast at her foretop was shortened and the rear superstructure extended slightly by having a single-storey housing erected upon it. This latter modification was extended further during the following year.

She underwent minor modifications during a refit in 1932, predominantly to the mast and foretop, before undertaking more goodwill trips around European ports.

In 1934, her crane was replaced, and two 8.8cm flak guns installed on the roof of her aft superstructure between turret 'Bruno' and the above-mentioned housing. Modifications were also made to her bridge structure.

In 1935 an aircraft catapult was added between the funnels, with an aircraft crane fitted to the port side, replacing the smaller derrick that had been located there. The derrick on the starboard side remained, however.

During the following year a pole mast was fitted to the rear face of the aft funnel and a twin 8.8cm flak unit on a triaxially stabilised mount replaced the two single 8.8cm guns on the aft superstructure. Two further units were added, one to either side of the housing on the aft superstructure, which was also extended and fitted with a rangefinder/fire control housing.

Königsberg underwent her final modifications in late 1939 when a degaussing coil was fitted around her hull just above the waterline.

Service

Königsberg, along with the light cruiser *Leipzig*, took part in the first German goodwill cruise to a British port since the end of World War One when they visited Portsmouth in 1934. Further modifications were carried out during the following year when *Königsberg* received an aircraft launch catapult, and again in 1936, after which the cruiser was allocated to the Gunnery Inspectorate for use as a training ship.

Like many other German warships, *Königsberg* took part in non-intervention patrolling during the Spanish Civil War, but her only real excitement during this period came when she was involved in forcing the release of a German steamer that had been seized by republican forces.

After her service in Spanish waters was completed, *Königsberg* returned to her assigned duties as a training ship, also being used as a test bed for some new radar equipment. After a further refit in 1939, the cruiser was designated as a target ship and allocated to the Unterseebootschule, a task that was cut short by the onset of war, when she was reassigned to the Aufklärungsstreitekräfte. Her first wartime task involved the laying of defensive minefields. On completion of these tasks she was sent to the Baltic to take part in training exercises before undergoing a further refit.

Königsberg did not return to active service until March 1940 when she was allocated to the forces designated for Operation Weserübung, the invasion of Norway. *Königsberg* was to transport over 600 soldiers of the Army's 69 Infanterie Division along with some shore-based naval artillerymen tasked with the capture of Bergen. On 8 April, the cruiser sailed from Wilhelmshaven along with *Köln* and a number of smaller vessels. In the early hours of 9 April she successfully transferred the first group of passengers to a number of E-boats and small launches

Königsberg is shown in this wartime picture in dry dock undergoing refitting work. Note the camouflage scheme, which has been applied to her hull and extending up onto her turrets.

A fine pre-war view of **Königsberg**, the ship in pristine condition with her crew mustered on the forecastle in their best white uniforms.

provided by the bigger ships for shuttling to the shore. Having disembarked part of her contingent of passengers, the cruiser then attempted to run for the port itself at speed, hoping to avoid the fire of Norwegian shore batteries. Luck was not on her side, however, and when passing through Byfjord on the approach to Bergen she was fired on by the 21cm guns of the Norwegian battery at Kvarven. The first shot was a near miss. The second was a direct hit on her starboard bow. She took second and third direct hits on her forecastle and suffered significant damage, with serious flooding and fire damage in her boiler rooms and electrical power generator rooms. *Königsberg* finally ended up drifting, her power out, and had to drop anchor. Eventually return fire from the heavy artillery of *Königsberg* and her sister *Köln*, supported by Luftwaffe bombers and the efforts of army troops on shore, silenced the shore batteries.

In need of repairs before she could be considered capable of putting to sea again, *Königsberg* was moored at the quay in such a position as to allow her full broadside to cover the approaches to the harbour in case of any attempt by the British to eject the German invasion force. Here, on the evening of 9 April, she survived an attack from British bombers without further damage.

Luck was about to run out for the light cruiser, however, and on the morning of the following day, as repair work on her continued, a further attack was launched by RAF Skua aircraft. Taken completely by surprise, the Germans had no opportunity to put up an effective flak defence. *Königsberg* was damaged by at least five 100lb bombs, one of which exploded between the quay and the ship's side, and another which passed through her decks, exiting and exploding in the water alongside, tearing a huge hole in her hull and killing several crew members. Three direct hits were received, one of which destroyed the auxiliary boiler room and two near misses in the water to her stern caused another huge rent in her hull.

The ship began listing heavily almost immediately. It was clear that there was no chance of saving her and the order was given to abandon ship. *Königsberg* was rolling over slowly, however, and the crew had plenty of time to evacuate, recovering the dead and wounded as well as large quantities of ammunition and essential equipment before she finally rolled over and sank just under three hours after the attack

Karlsruhe during training exercises in the calm waters of the Baltic. The almost negligible bow wave suggests she is moving at very low speed. That this is a pre-war scene is evidenced by the presence of her heraldic crest, adjacent to the anchor hawse. All such decorations were removed after the outbreak of war. Her aircraft is either not being carried, a common occurrence, or may have been launched. Her catapult is empty.

began. In 1941 the remains were refloated and salvaged, being gradually broken up for scrap.

KREUZER KARLSRUHE

KARLSRUHE SPECIFICATIONS

Length	169m
Beam	15.2m
Draught	5.7m
Maximum displacement	6.750 tons
Maximum speed	32 knots
Maximum endurance	5,700 nautical miles (turbines)
	8,000 nautical miles (diesels)
Main armament	9 x 15cm guns in three triple gun turrets
Secondary armament	12 x 10.5cm guns in six twin turrets
Flak armament	12 x 3.7cm guns in six twin turrets
	8 x 2cm guns on single mounts
Torpedoes	12 x 53.3cm torpedo tubes in four triple mounts
Aircraft	2 x Heinkel He 60 floatplanes
Complement	50 officers and 1,500 men

Ship's commanders

Fregattenkapitän Eugen Lindau	Nov 1929–Sep 1931
Kapitän zur See Erwin Wassner	Sep 1931–Dec 1932
Fregattenkapitän Wilhelm Harsdorf von Enderndorf	Dec 1932–Sep 1934
Kapitän zur See Günther Lütjens	Sep 1934–Sep 1935
Kapitän zur See Leopold Siemens	Sep 1935–Sep 1937
Kapitän zur See Erich Förste	Sep 1937–May 1938
Kapitän zur See Friedrich Rieve	Nov 1939–Apr 1940

General construction data

Karlsruhe was laid down at the Deutsche Werke yard in Kiel in July 1926, and launched just over a year later in August 1927. Completion and fitting-out work took a further two years, and the cruiser was finally commissioned into the Reichsmarine in November 1929.

Modifications

Karlsruhe was first modified over the winter of 1930–31. This involved shortening the pole mast attached to her foretop and adding additional housings on the roof of her aft superstructure and on the boat deck between her funnels.

The next series of significant modifications came in 1935 when a pole mast was fitted to the rear face of her aft funnel, and an aircraft catapult added between the funnels. An aircraft crane was also fitted on the port side, replacing the smaller derrick that had been sited here. Modifications were also made to the platforms on her battlemast. In July 1936 she underwent further modifications which mirrored those made to her older sister, namely the extending of the housing on her aft superstructure roof and the provision of a rangefinder/fire control unit on this structure, plus the replacement of her elderly single-

A fine shot looking back from the forecastle of *Karlsruhe*, giving a clear view of turret 'Anton', the forward rangefinders, and the battlemast with its searchlight platform, foretop and plethora of antennae.

barrelled 8.8cm flak guns with the three new twin 8.8cm housing sited as on *Königsberg*. Bridge wings were also added at this point.

In 1938 *Karlsruhe* underwent a major refit. The housing on her foretop was reduced to single storey and modifications made to the battlemast platforms. Raked funnel caps were fitted to both her funnels and the smaller starboard derrick was replaced by a larger crane. Searchlight platforms were added to each side of both of her funnels, her 8.8cm flak guns were replaced by heavier 10.5cm units, and a tripod mainmast fitted to the rear face of her aft funnel.

Modifications were also made to her anchor stowage. The older style hawse pipe opening on her starboard bow was deleted and an anchor cluse installed on the starboard side of her forecastle. Strangely, this modification was only carried out on the starboard side, the twin anchors to port remaining in a hawse pipe opening on the hull side.

Karlsruhe received her final major modification in 1940 when a degaussing coil was added.

Service

Following a period of trials in the Baltic, she was designated as a training ship and by May 1930 had set off on her first goodwill cruise into distant waters, calling at ports in Africa and South America. On her return to Germany, she took part in training exercises before setting off again on another goodwill cruise to the Americas. In all, she undertook five such long-distance cruises between 1930 and 1936, travelling as far as the Pacific and including Japan on her itinerary, with periods of training between each cruise. On the last cruise, *Karlsruhe* suffered severe damage during a tropical storm and was forced to call in at the US naval base at San Diego for running repairs.

On her return to Germany in June 1936, she went into dry dock for further repair works, modification and improvement work to her superstructure, and upgrading of her flak armament. On completion of this work and subsequent trials, she was called upon to serve on patrol duties off the coast of Spain during the Civil War but served only a few months in these waters before being recalled and thereafter spending the remainder of the year on further training exercises in the Baltic.

In May 1938 *Karlsruhe* was withdrawn from service and taken into the naval yards in Wilhelmshaven for an extensive refit and major modification work. She was recommissioned in November 1939 just after the outbreak of World War Two and spent the first few months of the conflict undergoing trials and training exercises. She was still not fully battleworthy by the launch of Operation Weserübung in April 1940, but it was nevertheless decided to use her in a troop transport role. She was to carry army infantry designated for the seizure of the port of Kristiansand, in the company of an E-boat tender also being used as a troop carrier, four torpedo boats (German torpedo boats were actually of similar size to a small destroyer) and a number of E-boats.

The group departed Bremerhaven on 8 April and initially made good progress, but by the time they reached the approaches to Kristiansand, the area was blanketed in thick fog, which made passage through the confined and treacherous waters of Kristiansand fjord very difficult. The German force was obliged to linger outside the immediate approach to the port until visibility improved on the morning of the next day. Kristiansand was protected by a number of heavy guns on the small island of Odderöy just outside the port itself and when

Karlsruhe comes into port to be met by a reception committee including a military band. Note that her crest is still in its original position, on the stem.

Karlsruhe began its final approach it came under heavy fire, the enemy shells landing uncomfortably close. *Karlsruhe* opened fire, but with the particular placement of turrets on her class of ship, could only bring the three guns of turret 'Anton' to bear. The cruiser would clearly place herself in considerable danger if she proceeded before this Norwegian fortress was neutralised, and the ship was therefore turned away so that she could bring her more powerful stern armament to bear. It soon became clear that the enemy could not be driven from this position by *Karlsruhe*'s guns alone.

The cruiser then stood off to a sufficient distance so that she could turn broadside on and bring all of her turrets to bear. This greater range would also allow a trajectory such as to have the cruiser's shells hit the enemy at a much more effective angle rather than the flatter trajectory achieved from her previous position. Some two hours after the first shots were fired, fog shrouded the port, forcing a halt to the action. An hour later this cleared and the order was given that two of the fast-moving torpedo boats land the troops they were carrying on Odderöy itself with orders to take out the Norwegian gun positions whilst *Karlsruhe* provided fire support. However, the defenders had decided to end their resistance and the Germans were able to enter the port unopposed. At just after noon, the Odderöy fortress also surrendered and *Karlsruhe* was able to disembark her passengers. Her task completed, she then headed for home, with three of the torpedo boats as escort.

Unfortunately for the Germans, lying in wait was the British submarine HMS *Truant*, which spotted the enemy group and fired off

An early shot of *Karlsruhe* negotiating the Kiel canal. Note that the flag being flown from her staff is that of the Reichsmarine with the Iron Cross in its centre. *Nürnberg* was the only cruiser to be commissioned directly into the later Kriegsmarine.

a spread of torpedoes. Despite zigzagging at speed, *Karlsruhe* was unable to avoid the torpedoes and was hit by two, one in the bows and another at the base of her mainmast. She immediately adopted a list and began to settle by the stern, shipping thousands of tons of water. Turbine and boiler rooms were flooded and electrical power was lost, resulting in the failure of the pumps in the torpedo-hit area to keep pace with the volume of water entering the damaged cruiser. Within minutes, the first officer had presented the captain with a very gloomy report on the ship's condition. Based on the report, it was decided that there was no hope of saving the ship and the order to abandon was given as she slowly settled in the water. The crew was taken on board one of the torpedo boats, which was then instructed to deliver the *coup de grâce* to her stricken companion.

A post-incident enquiry severely criticised the captain and first officer for not doing enough to try to save the ship. She was still afloat, albeit disabled, more than two hours after the torpedoes struck, and the pumps in the forward part of the ship were undamaged. Although these pumps were not capable of preventing the ship from flooding, they could have slowed down the volume of water entering her for some considerable time, suggesting that it may have been possible to tow her into port or to a spot where she may have been beached in shallow water. Indeed, it needed two torpedoes from the torpedo boat that administered the *coup de grâce* before the cruiser finally sank. Severe recriminations followed, many of which appear to have been fully justified. It certainly seems that nowhere near enough effort was made to save the damaged warship.

KREUZER KÖLN

KÖLN SPECIFICATIONS

Length	169m
Beam	15.2m
Draught	5.7m
Maximum displacement	6.750 tons
Maximum speed	32 knots
Maximum endurance	5,700 nautical miles (turbines)
	8,000 nautical miles (diesels)
Main armament	9 x 15cm guns in three triple gun turrets
Secondary armament	12 x 10.5cm guns in six twin turrets
Flak armament	12 x 3.7cm guns in six twin turrets
	8 x 2cm guns on single mounts
Torpedoes	12 x 53.3cm torpedo tubes in four triple mounts
Aircraft	2 x Heinkel He 60 floatplanes
Complement	50 officers and 1,500 men

General construction data

The keel of the third of the K-class cruisers was laid down at the Marinewerft at Wilhelmshaven in August 1926 and the ship launched in May 1928. On completion of her fitting out, *Köln* was commissioned into the Reichsmarine in January 1930, after which followed the usual period of trials and working up in the Baltic. The following year saw her take part in fleet manoeuvres as well as making a short goodwill cruise in the summer.

Modifications

Köln's first modifications, in 1931, followed those of her sisters. Housings were erected on the roof of her aft superstructure, between the funnels and forward of turret 'Bruno', the latter being provided with a rangefinder/fire control unit. Her original 8.8cm single flak units were replaced by twins and signal wings added to her bridge.

In 1935 modifications were made to her bridge deck and to the platform arrangement on her battlemast, an aircraft catapult added and the port derrick replaced by an aircraft crane. The aftmost housing on the rear superstructure was also extensively reworked and a raised circular platform added for a flak director position. A pole mast was also added to the rear face of the aft funnel.

An early photograph of the *Köln*. Note the aerial outriggers on the top of the second funnel and that no mainmast is featured.

An excellent later (though still pre-war) shot of *Köln*. Note the searchlight platforms on the derrick towers and the addition of the pole mast to the rear face of her second funnel. The number of platforms on her battlemast has been reduced.

Further modifications were made in 1937 when the aircraft catapult was removed and replaced by another housing similar to that which had been fitted earlier. The port aircraft crane was also removed and replaced by a simple derrick. During her winter 1940–41 refit, a degaussing coil was added and a helicopter landing pad added to the roof of turret 'Bruno'. Her final major modifications came in the spring of 1942 when a FuMO 21 radar set was installed in place of the forward rangefinder unit on the forward command-centre roof.

Very little in the way of augmentation to her flak armament seems to have been made to *Köln*, apart from the addition of single-barrelled 2cm flak guns on her forecastle.

Radar

Köln had a FuMO 24/25 set installed in August 1943. This was positioned on a small arm fitted to the face of the battlemast. On a further arm above this, was a FuMB 6 antenna. FuMB 4 antennae were also fitted on the side of the foretop.

Service

In 1932 she sailed into the Atlantic for further trials during the early spring before returning once again to the more familiar waters of the Baltic for further gunnery exercises. In the late part of that year, she sailed on her first world cruise with a compliment of officer cadets under training. Visiting ports in the Mediterranean, the Indian Ocean, the Pacific and Atlantic, she returned to Germany a full year later, her journey a great flag-waving success for Germany and its navy.

For the next two years, *Köln* was involved in a range of trials and training exercises in areas ranging from the Baltic to the North Sea and out into the mid-Atlantic, In early 1936, she was assigned to Fishery Protection duties. The summer of that year saw her, as with so many other German naval vessels, assigned to patrol duties in Spanish waters on the outbreak of the Civil War. It was *Köln* that transported the wounded crewmen from *Deutschland* home from Gibraltar to Germany after the latter ship had been bombed by republican aircraft off Ibiza.

Köln undertook a total of five patrols in Spanish waters after which she was again temporarily assigned to Fishery Protection duties in the North Sea before undergoing a refit at Kiel in the autumn of 1938. *Köln* was one of several ships that took part in the seizure of the Baltic port of Memel in March 1939, before joining in a major fleet exercise alongside the *Deutschland*, *Graf Spee*, *Admiral Scheer* and *Gneisenau* in Atlantic waters.

As the last few days before the outbreak of World War Two ticked away, *Köln* was once again operating in the Baltic and formed part of a blocking force intended to prevent any Polish warships escaping once the assault on the country was launched. In the event, this force was unsuccessful and many Polish warships did escape the clutches of the Germans. Thereafter, as with many of her counterparts, she was involved in laying large-scale defensive minefields in the approaches to German waters.

The K-class cruisers had a tendency to roll even in a moderate swell, as shown here. This view, looking astern from the bridge area, shows the ship's boats nearest the camera, a pinnace and the derrick with the searchlight platforms.

Thereafter, apart from an unsuccessful raiding sortie with *Gneisenau* and an escort mission along with *Leipzig* and *Nürnberg*, *Köln* had a rather uneventful few months until preparations were put in hand for Operation Weserübung, the invasion of Norway. For this mission, *Köln* was tasked along with her sister *Königsberg*, amongst others, with transporting army infantrymen who were to occupy the port of Bergen. Unlike her sister, *Köln* succeeded in reaching the harbour before the Norwegian shore batteries could react effectively. From here she was able to give fire support against the defences at Sandviken. Once her passengers were disembarked and the port was taken, *Köln* returned safely to Germany, escorted by two destroyers. No further operations were undertaken by the light cruisers during 1940 and at the end of

Köln is shown here wearing her so-called 'Baltic' camouflage in 1941. Note the dark area at the bow and the white-painted false bow wave. The broad black/white bands were painted across the hull and up over the superstructure.

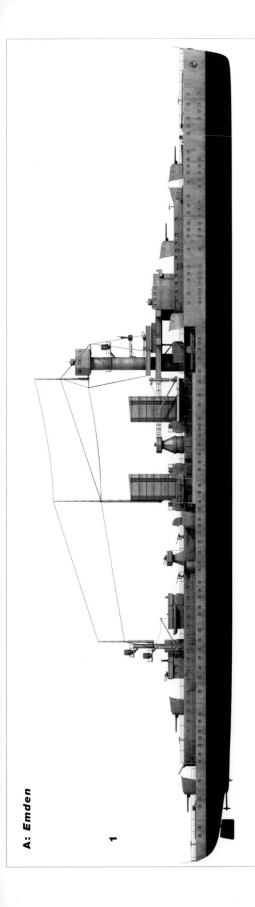

1

2

3

4

B: Königsberg

B

C: Leipzig

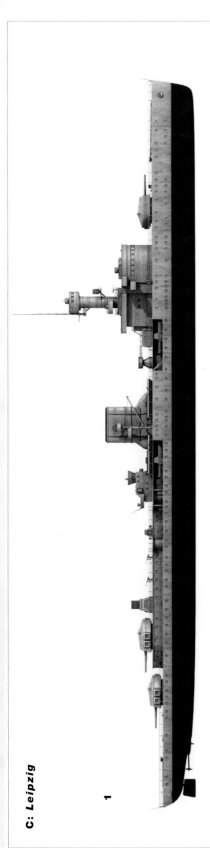

1

2

3

4

D: *NÜRNBERG CUTAWAY*

KEY

1 15cm triple gun turret 'Caesar'
2 15cm triple gun turret 'Bruno'
3 Exhaust vent
4 6m rangefinder
5 Flak fire control
6 Mainmast
7 Quad 2cm flak gun
8 4cm flak gun
9 Polemast abaft funnel
10 Searchlights
11 Funnel
12 Foremast
13 Foretop
14 Battlemast
15 FuMo 33 antenna
16 Admiral's bridge
17 4cm flak gun
18 Command bridge
19 2cm flak gun
20 Forward 25cm triple gun turret 'Anton'

21 Liferafts on turret sides
22 2cm flak gun
23 Lower ranks' accommodation
24 NCOs' accommodation
25 Ship's cutter
26 Ship's bakery
27 Ship's boats
28 Derrick
29 Forward triple torpedo tubes
30 8.8cm flak gun
31 Boiler rooms
32 Midships triple torpedo tubes
33 Turbine room
34 8.8cm flak gun
35 Turbine room
36 Diesel motor room
37 Propeller
38 Rudder

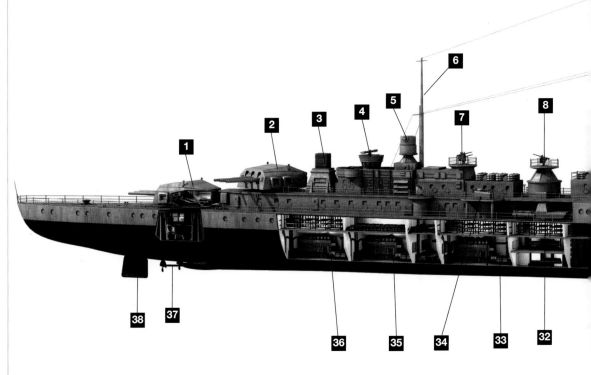

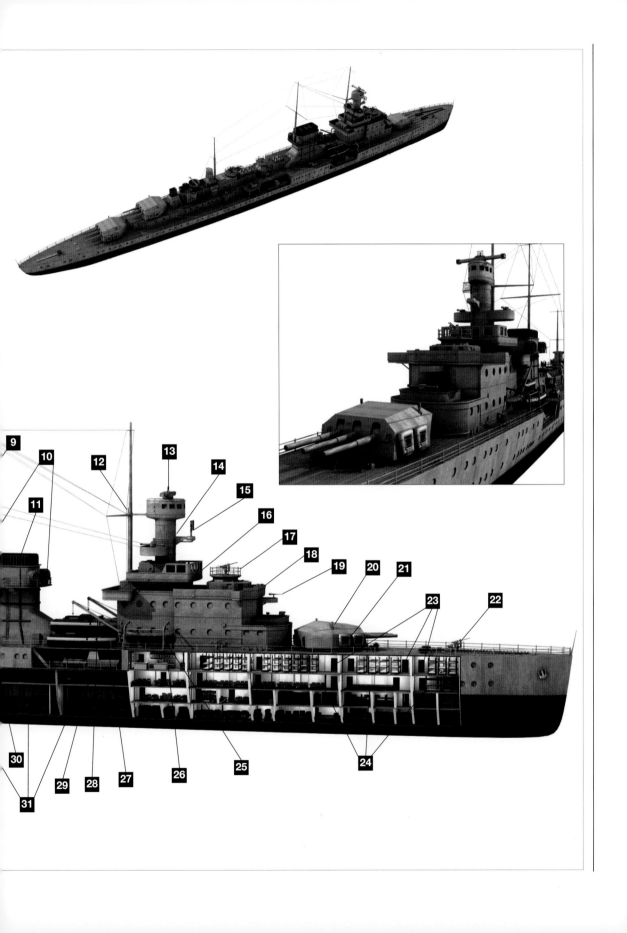

E **E: *Königsberg***

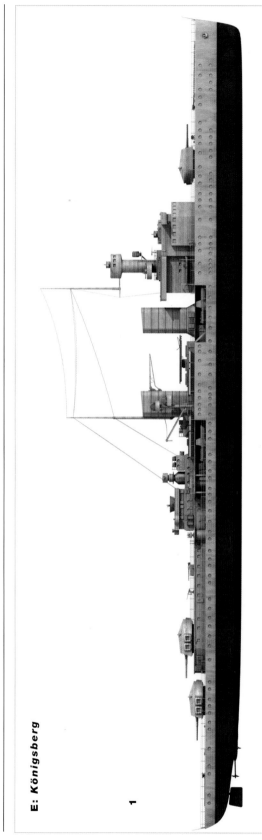

1

2

3

4

F: Emden

F

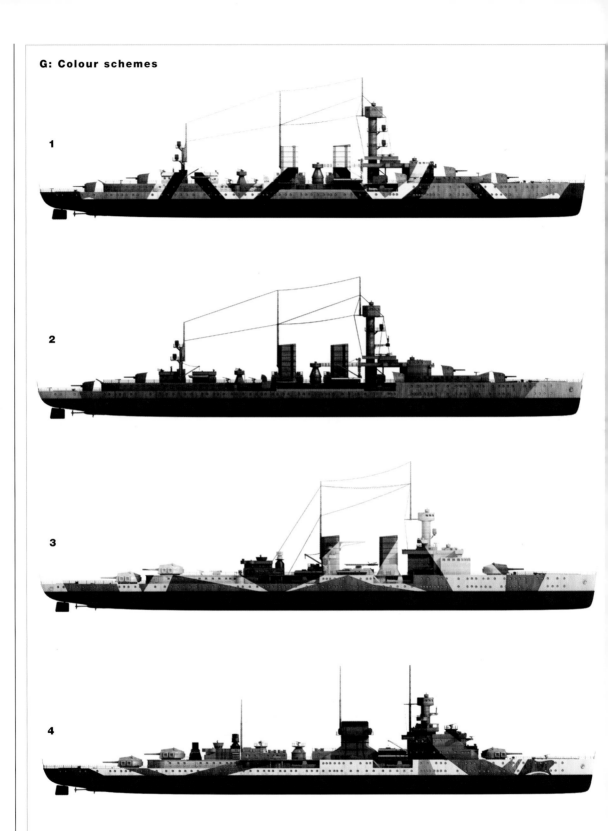

Köln after her bombing in 1945. The damage wrought by British bombs is clear to see. Note the tables and chairs set up on deck.

the year she entered dry dock for an extensive refit.

At this point, *Köln* became involved in historic trials for the use of shipboard helicopters. A special platform was erected on the roof of turret 'Bruno' and *Köln* took on board a Flettner 282 Kolibri helicopter, the world's first to enter formal military service. Trials were extremely successful, surpassing all expectations. The tiny helicopter even proved itself capable of evading attacking fighter aircraft. Trials ended in 1942, as far as *Köln* was concerned, but continued on other vessels.

Meanwhile, in September 1941, while still operating in the Baltic, *Köln* was involved in providing shore bombardment against Soviet positions on Dagö island, in support of a German landing, and during the following month was involved in the bombardment of Soviet positions on the island of Ristna. As the year progressed, however, severe winter weather conditions forced her return to port and subsequent transfer to duties in the North Sea following a further period in dry dock for overhaul and various structural modifications.

Köln sailed for Norwegian waters in mid-July, mooring at Narvik for a brief spell before moving on to Altafjord where, in fact, she did very little other than help keep up the German naval presence. In January 1943, *Köln* returned to Kiel where, on 17 February, she was taken out of service. She remained decommissioned for almost a full year. Only when the German fortunes on the Eastern Front suffered devastating reverses did the need for naval support in the east force her recommissioning. The cruiser was taken into dry dock once again for overhaul work required to make her ready for operational service, and work was finally completed on 1 July, at which point she was allocated to duty as a cadet training ship.

Her first significant operation thereafter was a minelaying mission that had to be abandoned before it even took place, due to RAF bombing raids on her moorings in Oslofjord. Thereafter she took part in a few minor escort runs. A major air raid in December, though it did not score any direct hits on the cruiser, achieved several near misses that were enough to cause damage to her engines, rendering her unfit for service. The local repair facilities were unable to completely repair the damage and so *Köln* was ordered to return to Germany, reaching Wilhelmshaven in early January. Over the next few months, the dockyard was subjected to numerous bombing raids by the RAF and finally, on 30

March, *Köln* itself was hit, took on a serious list and gradually settled, on an even keel, in the shallow water of the dock.

As the cruiser was still basically intact, though partially submerged and unable to move, it was decided to use her as a static gun battery and her main armament turrets were put into action to give fire support against enemy tanks approaching Wilhelmshaven. She was used in this role until hostilities ceased. After the end of the war, the wreck was partially broken up and in 1956, 11 years after the end of the war, the remnants were finally raised and scrapped.

THE *LEIPZIG*-CLASS CRUISERS

This class, of which only two examples were built, was broadly similar in appearance to the K class, at least in original form. The principal obvious difference was that both of these vessels were somewhat larger than the K class, and had only a single funnel. *Nürnberg* featured a much more heavily developed bridge superstructure unlike any of the other light cruisers. *Leipzig*'s forward superstructure resembled far more closely that of the K class. One further difference, though not immediately apparent in photos, especially those from a broadside aspect, is that the aft main armament turrets of these later cruisers were mounted on the centreline and not offset like their earlier counterparts.

These cruisers were driven by three shafts rather than the two of *Emden* and the K class. For *Nürnberg*, each of the main shafts was driven by a single high-pressure turbine and two low-pressure turbines, all manufactured by Deutsche Werke of Kiel. In *Leipzig*'s case, each main shaft was driven by one high-pressure and one low-pressure turbine, all built by Krupp. In both cases, the central shaft was powered by four MAN two-stroke seven-cylinder diesels. The flexibility offered by this arrangement was not without its costs. If one or the other system was in use, and it was required to bring both systems into use, all engines had to be stopped for several minutes before the systems could be double-coupled.

In both ships, the turbines were fed by six oil-fired boilers, arranged in three boiler rooms each, with one boiler to port and one to starboard. The cruisers were steered by the use of a single rudder. Electrical power was provided by two 250kW turbo generators and two 90kW diesel generators.

A fine study of the *Leipzig*, showing her in considerable detail. She is immediately distinguishable from the K class by her single funnel. This is a pre-war shot, but taken some time after 1935, as her flag is the Reichskriegsflagge of the Kriegsmarine, not the flag of the earlier Reichsmarine into which she was first commissioned.

KREUZER LEIPZIG

LEIPZIG SPECIFICATIONS

Length	177m
Beam	16.3m
Draught	5.7m
Maximum displacement	8,427 tons
Maximum speed	32 knots (turbines)
	16.5 knots (diesels)
Maximum endurance	3,780 nautical miles
Main armament	9 x 15cm guns in three triple gun turrets
Secondary armament	12 x 10.5cm guns in six twin turrets
Flak armament	12 x 3.7cm guns in six twin turrets
	8 x 2cm guns on single mounts
Torpedoes	12 x 53.3cm torpedo tubes in four triple mounts
Aircraft	2 x Heinkel He 60 floatplanes
Complement	24 officers and 826 men

Ship's commanders

Kapitän zur See Hans-Herbert Stobwasser	Oct 1931–Sep 1933
Korvettenkapitän Otto Hormel	Sep 1933–Sep 1935
Fregattenkapitän Otto Schenk	Sep 1935–Oct 1937
Kapitän zur See Werner Löwisch	Oct 1937–Apr 1939
Kapitän zur See Heinz Nordmann	Apr 1939–Feb 1940
Kapitän zur See Werner Stichling	Dec 1940–Aug 1942
Kapitän zur See Friedrich-Traugott Schmidt	Aug 1942–Sep 1942
Kapitän zur See Waldemar Winther	Sep 1942–Feb 1943
Decommissioned	Feb 1943
Recommissioned	Aug 1943
Kapitän zur See Walter Hülsemann	Oct 1943–Aug 1944
Kapitän zur See Heinrich Spörel	Aug 1944–Nov 1944
Korvettenkapitän Hagen Küster	Nov 1944–Jan 1945
Korvettenkapitän Walter Bach	Jan 1945–May 1945

General construction data

The keel of *Leipzig* was laid in April 1928 at the Marinewerft in Wilhelmshaven and the vessel launched in October 1929. Completion and fitting out took two more years and the new cruiser was commissioned into the Reichsmarine in October 1931.

Modifications

Leipzig's first major modification came in late 1934 when the housing on the superstructure roof between the funnel and the battlemast was removed and replaced by an aircraft catapult. An aircraft crane also replaced her port derrick at this time. As with the K-class cruisers, her original 8.8cm single flak gun fittings were replaced by twin units.

In 1940 a degaussing cable was fitted and in 1941 her aircraft catapult and the aftmost pair of torpedo tube mounts were removed. In 1943, the forward torpedo tube mounts were also removed. At the same time, however, she was fitted with a FuMO 24/25 radar antenna on a new platform replacing the searchlight platform on her battlemast. A further platform just below her foretop now carried a FuMB 6 set. This was to be the last major modification/improvement to the cruiser. None of the planned major improvements to *Leipzig*'s flak armament appear to have come to fruition.

Service

Throughout 1932 and into 1933, *Leipzig* undertook extensive training in the Baltic as well as making a number of overseas goodwill cruises. 1934 saw Leipzig making a goodwill visit to Portsmouth. At the end of that year she went into Kiel for major modifications and in the spring of 1935 took part in major fleet manoeuvres with *Köln, Deutschland* and *Schlesien*. Later in that year, during further fleet manoeuvres, *Leipzig* received a visit from the head of state, Adolf Hitler.

In the spring of 1936, *Leipzig* exercised in the Atlantic with *Nürnberg* and *Köln* before making further courtesy visits to foreign ports. In August of that year, she was assigned to non-intervention patrolling off the coast of Spain during the Civil War, completing several patrols between August 1936 and June 1937. On her return from Spanish waters, *Leipzig* entered the Baltic where she spent the remainder of that year on training exercises.

The following year was also taken up predominantly with training exercises in Baltic waters before the cruiser went into dock for major modifications, not emerging until March 1939, just in time to take part in the return of the Baltic port of Memel to the Reich.

A shot of *Leipzig* taken from waterline level off her bow shows to good effect the large heraldic shield. The layout of her bow anchors, with two to port and one to starboard, is also clearly seen.

In mid-April, *Leipzig* sailed out into the Atlantic with *Deutschland*, *Gneisenau*, and a strong force of destroyers and U-boats for grand-scale naval exercises lasting around one month. The remaining months of peace before the outbreak of World War Two were taken up with further large-scale naval exercises. On the outbreak of hostilities, *Leipzig* was part of the blocking force formed to prevent the breakout of Polish naval vessels from the Baltic, an exercise that was to prove unsuccessful.

Following this rather futile exercise, *Leipzig* transferred to the North Sea and, like the other light cruisers, was involved in laying mass defensive minefields, a task lasting through to the end of September, after which she moved into the Baltic for extensive exercises.

Leipzig's next mission, in late November, involved escorting the battleships *Gneisenau* and *Scharnhorst* through the Skagerrak as they departed on their war patrol, then carrying out contraband patrolling in this area whilst she waited to escort the bigger ships home again at the end of their mission four days later.

Leipzig continued such escort missions through the remainder of the year, but her luck ran out on 13 December when, tasked with escorting a group of destroyers and smaller warships returning from a minelaying mission, together with *Nürnberg*, and the K-class cruiser *Köln*, she was torpedoed by the British submarine HMS *Salmon*. At 1125hrs, just as a pair of Heinkel He 115 floatplanes arrived to provide air cover, a torpedo struck her below the waterline at one of the bulkheads separating two of her boiler rooms. The Heinkel had spotted the torpedo tracks and flashed a 'U...U...U' (for U-boat) warning to the cruiser, but ironically the letter 'U' was also the recognition code for the day and the signal was misinterpreted by the cruiser as a simple recognition code. The power of the explosion damaged *Leipzig's* keel and deformed her armoured deck. Bulkheads were ruptured and all steam and fuel lines on the port side were fractured. Two of her three boiler rooms flooded and the port turbine ceased operating. The remaining intact boiler room was little better off, filling with acrid smoke and also taking in water. Over 1,700 tons of water flooded into the cruiser's shattered hull. Fire control for her armament and communications equipment was rendered inoperable by electrical power failures.

Nürnberg too was hit by a British torpedo and as *Leipzig's* speed rapidly fell off, was soon lost from sight. Assistance was requested and at 1315hrs air cover arrived, followed shortly afterwards by the reappearance of both *Nürnberg* and *Köln*. With her turbine engines uncoupled, Leipzig was able to make headway on her diesel-powered central shaft.

It appears that the British submarine may have deliberately intended to damage two, rather than sink one cruiser. The German cruisers were certainly left in a perilous situation. In the time it took them to get under way again, and with no escort vessels present, the enemy submarine might well have had time to reload and return to finish them off.

Fifteen minutes later, two destroyers arrived to provide an escort into Brunsbüttel for the damaged cruisers. Early next morning more escorts arrived but at this point the force was split, *Köln* being directed to sail for

This photo was taken from immediately behind turret 'Bruno', looking forward, and shows the twin flak mount which replaced the earlier two individual single-barrelled 8.8cm flak guns which were originally sited here. Note the foul weather gear worn by the crewman.

Wilhelmshaven. Fate had not yet finished with *Leipzig's* group, however, and at 1235hrs, with the German ships only 30 miles from the mouth of the Elbe river, the escort off her starboard bow was hit by a torpedo launched by yet another lurking British submarine. It was at first thought she had run into a mine but a further torpedo track was spotted making for *Leipzig*. Fortunately, this second torpedo passed ahead of *Leipzig's* bows, the submarine having overestimated her speed. It is presumed the enemy submarine must have dived deep to avoid countermeasures and make her escape as no further torpedoes appear to have been fired, and by early evening, the force finally arrived at Brunsbüttel.

Leipzig was immediately directed into the Deutsche Werke yard for repairs. Whilst still undergoing repairs, *Leipzig* was decommissioned and downgraded to the status of a training ship. Four of her boilers were removed and the resultant space used to create additional on-board accommodation. She was eventually recommissioned at the end of 1940 but still remained a training ship. Of course, the removal of the boilers had an adverse effect on her top speed, resulting in her never again being able to attain her designed performance levels.

Her next operational mission came in early June 1941, when she was part of the escort that accompanied the pocket battleship (now reclassified as a heavy cruiser) *Lützow*, into Norwegian waters.

Following her return from this mission, *Leipzig* was assigned to the Baltic where she operated in the southern sector alongside *Emden*. The two cruisers were involved in providing heavy artillery support for German army units assaulting Soviet positions. *Leipzig* returned to Kiel in October and spent the remainder of the year exercising with the *Admiral Scheer*. In 1942, *Leipzig* spent the entire year on training exercises in the Baltic, as flagship of the commander of the training fleet.

A close-up of *Leipzig*'s Heinkel He 60 floatplane sitting in its launch cradle on the catapult, just ahead of the funnel. The aircraft is in its pre-war pale grey livery. The biplane He 60 was later replaced by the far superior Arado Ar 196.

In March 1943 *Leipzig* was decommissioned once again, but this situation lasted only a few months, as the reverses Germany was now suffering on the Eastern Front meant that every ship was required. On 1 August, she was again recommissioned though overhaul, repairs, training, the replacement of worn-out gun barrels and installation of radar equipment meant that it was some time before she was once again ready for operational use. A further delay in reaching combat readiness was caused by an outbreak of meningitis on board, which resulted in the deaths of two crewmen. Finally, in mid-September 1944, she carried out convoy escort exercises in the Baltic with *Admiral Scheer* before beginning operational escort duty for troop transport convoys running between Gotenhafen and Swinemünde.

A stern view of *Leipzig*. The boom shown just astern of turret 'Caesar' is intended to avoid damage to the ship's propellers whilst in port, preventing her hullside swinging in against the quayside.

On 14 October 1944, *Leipzig* was moored at Gotenhafen. Orders had been received to sail for Swinemünde to load up with mines. At 1745hrs, *Leipzig* departed, running at slow speed on her central diesel engine. A signal had been received warning that the heavy cruiser *Prinz Eugen* was inbound for Gotenhafen. Unfortunately, due to a breakdown in communications on board, neither the first officer nor navigation officer was informed. As *Leipzig*'s main boilers were brought up to full steam and preparations

were made to decouple the diesel and transfer to turbine drive, confusion over which channel *Leipzig* should follow led to her being out of position when the *Prinz Eugen* loomed out of the mist. In her correct channel and doing fully 20 knots, she slammed into *Leipzig's* port side just ahead of the funnel. 39 crewmen were killed or injured. The two ships were wedged together until the afternoon of 16 October. *Leipzig* was towed carefully into Gotenhafen where she went into the floating dry dock. It was clear that damage to the cruiser was so serious that proper repairs were not considered viable and accordingly only such repairs as were required to keep her afloat and allow her limited movement were carried out.

In March 1945, as Red Army units approached Gotenhafen, *Leipzig's* guns were put to good use in providing fire support for German units conducting a fighting withdrawal. With the fall of Gotenhafen imminent, on 24 March *Leipzig* moved to Hela and embarked as many refugees as she could carry, then sailed westwards, able to make at best only 6 knots. Fighting off attacks from Soviet aircraft and avoiding at least two torpedo attacks by enemy submarines, she reached the safety of Denmark on 29 April.

At the end of hostilities, the ship was in such poor condition that no further use could be found for her other than as an accommodation hulk for those involved in the post-war clearing of mines from coastal waters by the German Minesweeping Administration under British control. Eventually, in July 1946, the hulk was towed out to sea and scuttled.

KREUZER NÜRNBERG

NÜRNBERG SPECIFICATIONS

Length	181m
Beam	16.4m
Draught	5.8m
Maximum displacement	9,040 tons
Maximum speed	32 knots (turbines)
	16.5 knots (diesels)
Maximum endurance	3,780 nautical miles (turbines)
Main armament	9 x 15cm guns in three triple gun turrets
Secondary armament	12 x 10.5cm guns in six twin turrets
Flak armament	12 x 3.7cm guns in six twin turrets
	8 x 2cm guns on single mounts
Torpedoes	12 x 53.3cm torpedo tubes in four triple mounts
Aircraft	2 x Heinkel He 60 floatplanes
Complement	26 officers and 870 men

Ship's commanders

Kapitän zur See Hubert Schmundt	Nov 1935–Oct 1936
Kapitän zur See Theodor-Heinrich Riedel	Oct 1936–Oct 1937
Kapitän zur See Walter Krastel	Oct 1937–Nov 1938
Kapitän zur See Heinz Degenhardt	Nov 1938–Dec 1938
Kapitän zur See Otto Klüber	Dec 1938–Aug 1940
Kapitän zur See Leo Kreisch	Aug 1940–Mar 1941

Kapitän zur See Ernst von Studnitz	Mar 1941–Jun 1943
Decommissioned	1943
Recommissioned	May 1943
Kapitän zur See Gerhardt Böhmig	Jun 1943–Oct 1944
Kapitän zur See Helmuth Geissler	Oct 1944–May 1945

The *Nürnberg*. Although very similar to Leipzig, there are a number of distinguishing features, the most obvious of which is her much larger bridge/forward superstructure and the siting of her aircraft catapult astern of, rather than forward of, the funnel.

General construction data

Nürnberg's keel was laid at the Deutsche Werft in Kiel in November 1933. Construction took just over one year, with the cruiser being launched in December 1934. On completion, she was commissioned into the Kriegsmarine in November 1935.

Modifications

Not being completed until 1935, many of the improvements that were carried out to her predecessors were incorporated into *Nürnberg* during her construction. Her first significant modification came in March 1941 when she had a FuMO 21 radar set installed in place of the 6m forward rangefinder. In early 1942 her aircraft catapult was removed and her radar equipment upgraded to a FuMO 25 set, but mounted on a platform on the face of the battlemast and with the forward rangefinder reinstated. In 1944 a FuMO 63 set was installed on a mount on the mainmast.

Nürnberg was the only light cruiser to have been given significant additional flak armament. *Flakvierling* were installed on the roof of turret 'Bruno' and on the roof of the navigating bridge, and the number of 2cm single-barrelled units was also increased. The *Flakvierling* on the roof of the navigating bridge was replaced in 1944 by a more powerful 4cm Flak 28, and a second example of this weapon installed on the tower, which had previously supported the aircraft catapult after the latter feature had been removed. An additional 2cm single-barrelled unit was also installed around this time, together with five twin 2cm mounts.

Radar

Nürnberg was initially provided with a FuMO 21 set in 1941. This was positioned in place of the forward 6m rangefinder on the roof of the forward command centre. In 1944, this was removed and a 2cm quad *Flakvierling* positioned in its place. In place of the FuMO 21, *Nürnberg* was provided with a FuMO 24/25 set, and a FuMB 6 in similar layout to that

A fine study of the light cruiser prior to the outbreak of war. Note the accommodation ladders let down from the deck adjacent to the torpedo launcher positions, suggesting she is moored just out of harbour. In fact the chain of the single starboard anchor can just be seen at the other side of the bow.

on *Leipzig*. In addition, a FuMO 63 was fitted to the mainmast.

Service

Her first few months of service were spent exercising in the Baltic. In April 1936, the cruiser exercised in Atlantic waters with *Köln* and *Leipzig* before returning to the Baltic, still with her cruiser companions, for further training. On the outbreak of the Spanish Civil War, *Nürnberg* was assigned to patrol duties in Spanish waters, and completed four such patrols during this conflict, none of which involved her in any significant action.

In September 1937, *Nürnberg* was involved in major fleet exercises with the pocket battleships *Deutschland* and *Admiral Graf Spee* as well as *Karlsruhe* and *Leipzig* and numerous destroyers and smaller craft before returning to dock for refitting. Returning to sea in January 1938, *Nürnberg* spent the first three months of the year undergoing more exercises in the Baltic before undertaking a further refit. A short training cruise in June/July took her to Norway after which she once again sailed for the Baltic and intensive training exercises with other units of the fleet. In 1939 *Nürnberg* was part of the naval force that was involved in the return of the port of Memel to the Reich.

On the outbreak of war, *Nürnberg* formed part of the blocking force intended to prevent the breakout of Polish warships from the Baltic. The exercise was no great success and several Polish destroyers and submarines escaped. Like her fellow cruisers, she also took part in the huge operation laying defensive minefields in the approaches to German waters. Thereafter, she returned to the Baltic yet again for exercises with *Leipzig*. In November and December she was employed on escort duties, providing cover for destroyer units returning from offensive minelaying operations in British waters.

On 12 December 1939, whilst steaming with *Leizpig* and *Köln* to a rendezvous point with a force of five destroyers which were returning from a minelaying mission, the German cruiser force was attacked by the British submarine HMS *Salmon*. Hits were scored on both *Leipzig* and *Nürnberg*. In *Nürnberg*'s case, she was hit forward on the starboard side, right at the bow. The submarine was seen on the surface shortly thereafter but dived again and disappeared after *Nürnberg* opened fire on her. The cruiser was not

The appearance of a large warship at any mooring is usually a great attraction for curious civilians. Here, *Nürnberg* has drawn her share of admiring onlookers.

too seriously damaged, and it was quickly established that the watertight bulkheads in the forward part of the ship were holding. Just under an hour later, however, a further attack occurred, this time by British aircraft. Fortunately, none of the bombs dropped hit their target and *Nürnberg* suffered no further damage.

Three of the destroyers that the cruisers had been dispatched to escort arrived on the scene around two hours after the attack. As *Nürnberg* was not seriously damaged, she was dispatched from the rest of the force and ordered to make her own way home with only one of these destroyers in attendance. The cruiser reached home waters in the evening of that same day. She was immediately taken into dry dock for repairs and was out of service until the beginning of June, undergoing repairs and modifications.

Nürnberg's bow, showing the damage she suffered in the torpedo attack on 1939. Fortunately, her internal bulkheads held and she was able to return safely to harbour. Note that her heraldic shield is still in place, suggesting it was some little time *after* the outbreak of war before these insignia were removed from all ships.

On completion of this work, *Nürnberg* was dispatched to Norway where she was involved in escort duties for troop convoys and also, at one point, as escort for the battleship *Gneisenau*. During this period in Norway *Nürnberg* was part of a powerful German squadron including the *Prinz Eugen*, *Admiral Hipper*, *Lützow*, *Deutschland*, *Emden* and *Köln*. She saw no action, being held in reserve for use in Operation Seelöwe, the proposed invasion of Great Britain. In the event, of course, this never took place and in early 1941 *Nürnberg* found herself downgraded to the status of a training ship, with no plans for operational use.

This changed, however, following the German invasion of the Soviet Union in June 1941. *Nürnberg* was recalled and formed part of a blocking force, along with *Tirpitz* and *Köln*, to prevent any attempt by the Soviet fleet units in Kronstadt to flee. By October, however, she was back in her training role. She remained in this role until late November 1942 when she was once again recalled for operational use and dispatched to Norway to replace *Admiral Scheer*, which was being recalled to Germany for overhaul. *Nürnberg* reached Norway on 2 December but saw no active service, and once her presence was no longer required she reverted to the status of a training ship.

Like her light cruiser counterparts, *Nürnberg* was once more recalled to operational service in 1944 as Germany's military fortunes waned. Initially, she was used on convoy escort duties, before being assigned to minelaying in Norwegian waters. By January 1945, she was lying in port in Copenhagen where severe shortages of fuel rendered her inoperative. Here, her last shots in anger were fired when members of her crew beat off an attempt by Danish resistance fighters to seize the ship on 5 May. British forces arrived in the Danish port on the following day and matters calmed down. On 22 May the cruiser was ordered by the British

to sail to Wilhelmshaven. Here she was handed over to the Soviet Union on 2 January 1946. Commissioned into the Soviet navy as the *Admiral Makarov*, she served for several more years as a training ship. She was finally scrapped in 1960, having survived longer than any other significant German warship.

An opportunistic photographer snapped this shot of *Nürnberg* through a window as she passed through the Kiel Canal. It shows to advantage the bizarre but effective Baltic pattern camouflage.

CONCLUSION

Of all the major German warship classes, the light cruisers were probably the least successful. Even during the pre-war years, when all that was expected of them was to carry cadets on international goodwill cruises, they experienced severe problems in their seaworthiness. They were simply too flimsy for use on the world's major oceans. As far as their combat use was concerned, their record was less than impressive:

Emden Apart from minor shore bombardment and minelaying duties, *Emden* spent most of her career as a training ship.

Königsberg Bombed and sunk in 1940.

Karlsruhe Torpedoed and sunk in 1940.

Köln Shore bombardment, minelaying and training duties, bombed and sunk 1945.

Leipzig Torpedoed 1939, repaired, shore bombardment, training and minelaying duties. Rammed by *Prinz Eugen*, 1944. Further shore bombardment work in 1945.

Nürnberg Torpedoed 1939, repaired, escort and minesweeping duties. Survived the war to be handed over to the Soviet Union.

Probably the greatest service was given by *Leipzig* in her shore bombardment work in the Baltic in 1945, where her efforts were greatly appreciated by the retreating German armies.

BIBLIOGRAPHY

Breyer, Siegfried, and Koop, Gerhard, *The German Navy at War 1939–45, Volume 1, The Battleships*, Schiffer Publishing, West Chester, 1989

Gröner, Erich, *Die deutschen Kriegsschiffe 1835–1945*, J.F. Lehmanns, Munich, 1968

Harnack, Wolfgang, and Sonntag, Dietrich, *Kreuzer Nürnberg*, Verlag E.S. Mittler & Sohn GmbH, Hamburg 1998

Koop, Gerhard, and Schmolke, Klaus-Peter, *German Light Cruisers of World War II*, Greenhill Books, London, 2002

Mallmann- Showell, Jak P., *Kriegsmarine Handbook*, Sutton Publishing, Stroud, 1999

Whitley, M.J., *German Cruisers of World War Two*, Arms and Armour Press, London, 1985

COLOUR PLATE COMMENTARY

A: *EMDEN*

1 *Emden* in her wartime configuration, circa 1942. Note the considerable difference in the appearance of her foretop, and also the enlarged deckhouse structures on her after deck. The second funnel has been raised to the same height as the first and the mainmast has been reduced. Her appearance now shows the effect of five years of war use and she is heavily weathered. A pole mast has been attached to the rear of the second funnel and her mainmast reduced.

2 Very soon after completion, it was found that the fire control position on *Emden*'s foretop was unacceptably cramped. A new foremast was fitted with an enlarged foretop fire control position.

3 *Emden*'s mainmast was also heavily redesigned, and shortened to little more than a support pole for two searchlight positions. This was carried out during her major refit of 1933–34.

4 Prior to the outbreak of war *Emden* carried, as well as the usual ship's crest on the side of her bow, a large Iron Cross on the stem, commemorating the original *Emden*, lost in battle with the cruiser HMAS *Sydney*.

B: *KÖNIGSBERG*

This plate shows the light cruiser *Königsberg* during Operation Weserübung, the invasion of Norway. Tied up at the quay in the harbour at Bergen, she has come under attack from British Skua aircraft. The attack came as a complete surprise but *Königsberg*'s flak is putting up as heavy a barrage as it can. Unlike the enhanced level of flak weaponry that was provided to the light cruisers later in the war, in 1940, *Königsberg* carried six 8.8cm twin flak guns, plus four twin 3.7cm guns and eight single-barrelled 2cm guns. Due to her position alongside the quay, the flak guns on her starboard side would be unlikely to be able to be brought to bear on the attackers. The Skuas were armed with 100lb bombs, one of which has exploded between the quay and the cruiser's hull. Another has passed clean through her before exploding in the water and holing her

ABOVE **A midships view of *Nürnberg* after the outbreak of war shows the Heinkel He 60 floatplane in its new dark green livery. These aircraft were crewed by Luftwaffe rather than naval personnel.**

BELOW **Against a background of high Norwegian peaks, the effectiveness of *Nürnberg*'s disruptive pattern camouflage can be appreciated. This was one of several schemes she is known to have worn.**

Nürnberg. This midships view shows her in her post-war guise as the Soviet *Admiral Makarov*. The ship is decked out with bunting and the flak guns are firing a salute to mark a visit by Egyptian President Gamal Abdel Nasser.

BELOW Clearly visible in this post-refit view of *Königsberg* is the new aircraft crane, which had been fitted to her port side in place of the original small derrick.

below the waterline. Three have scored direct hits on her and others have exploded in the water near her stern, ripping open her plates there as well. With flames raging amidships, the cruiser is developing a list to port. Fortunately, although the damage to the cruiser was fatal, she settled relatively slowly, giving the crew time to evacuate the ship and also to unload much of her ammunition and essential equipment. At 1051hrs on 10 April 1940, *Königsberg* finally rolled over and sank. 41 crewmembers were killed or injured, mercifully light casualties from a crew of well over 600. She was later raised and towed out of the harbour to be cut up for scrap.

C: *LEIPZIG*

1 and 2 These illustrations show the light cruiser *Leipzig* as she was constructed. Instantly identifiable as distinct from the K Class by her single rather than twin funnels. At this stage she has no provision for an aircraft and no radar equipment fitted. Note the two single-barrel 8.8cm flak guns

ahead of turret 'Bruno'. She is in the standard pale grey livery of the period.

3 In 1935, *Leipzig* was taken into port and had the deckhouse forward of the funnel removed to facilitate the addition of a catapult for a Heinkel He 60 seaplane. This view shows the funnel area and the searchlight platforms fitted to the crane pillars. The catapult was removed in 1941 after her relegation to second-line duties.

4 In the latter part of her career, *Leipzig* had FuMO 25 and FuMB radar antennae fitted to her mainmast, following the removal of the searchlight platform.

D: *NÜRNBERG* CUTAWAY

As the cutaway of *Nürnberg* shows, her basic layout was fairly conventional. The greatest part of the ship's innards, from the base of the battlemast through to the stern, was taken up by the various engine-room compartments. Immediately below the funnel area were the three boiler rooms, each with two boilers. Further aft were the magazines for the

Passing through the Kiel Canal was a popular place for warships to be photographed. Here *Nürnberg* passes beneath the Levensauer Hochbrüche bridge. Her heralidc crest, displaying a large German eagle, can be made out at the bow.

BELOW This fine shot of the light cruiser *Emden* clearly shows the unusual layout of her main armament. The single gun turrets forward and aft are conventional enough, but note the additional turrets just abaft the second funnel and above the torpedo tubes, which are inset into recesses in the hull side.

8.8cm flak ammunition on the starboard side and a storeroom on the port. Next came the forward turbine room containing the turbine driving the starboard shaft, followed by the gearing rooms, port and starboard. Then followed the aft turbine room, containing the turbine driving the port shaft. Moving further aft was the diesel engine room containing the four large MAN diesels driving the centre shaft.

Forward of the boiler rooms was the pump room and radio room followed by the forward generator space, above which sat further 8.8cm flak ammunition storage and the command centre. Forward of this, under turret 'Anton' lay the 15cm ammunition and torpedo warhead storage as well as the ship's refrigerated storage area. The furthest forward area was taken up with fuel oil stores and, right in the bow, the engineering workshop.

The next deck level above the engine room, in the bow, was taken up by the ship's naval and clothing stores. This was followed by crew space and junior NCOs' mess areas. Thereafter, almost the full length of the ship on this level was taken up with crew accommodation. The upper deck level forward was taken up with further crew accommodation and, just under the battlemast, the crew's galley. Moving further towards the stern on this level, immediately under the funnel, were the crew's bathroom/showers and the auxiliary boiler room.

Under the pedestal column for the aircraft catapult sat the officer's galley. From this point on towards the stern the first level of the aft superstructure was given over to officer-rank accommodation and admiral's quarters, apart from the final two compartments, which contained the officers' and senior NCOs' heads.

The deckhouses on the roof of the aft superstructure contained the cooks' mess and further offices and accommodation. Immediately forward of the funnel was the ship's laundry, whilst the forward superstructure, as well as the bridge itself, contained further officer-rank accommodation.

The ship's launches sit in cradles just forward of the funnel, and were lifted in and out of the water by cranes sited at the rear of the bridge deck. The ship's boats sit just forward of this, suspended on davits.

Here *Nürnberg* is wearing the camouflage scheme she sported in 1941. She has the FuMO 21 radar set installed, which replaced the original forward 6m rangefinder.

Nürnberg, being the last of the light cruisers to be constructed, was the best protected, featuring the latest developments in armour plating, Krupp Pz240 nickel steel protection.

E: *KÖNIGSBERG*

1 This view shows the light cruiser *Königsberg* after her 1939–40 refit, with an aircraft catapult installed between the funnels. Her port derrick has been replaced by an aircraft crane, and an extended pole mast fitted to the rear of her second funnel. Both funnels now have small raked caps fitted and searchlight platforms fitted either side. Her foretop has

been significantly remodelled and the anchor moved from a hawse hole on the hull side to a cluse on the forecastle.

Additional 2cm flak guns have also been installed in the forecastle and quarterdeck.

2 *Königsberg*'s aircraft catapult was installed between her two funnels.

3 The standard aircraft carried by those light cruisers fitted with catapults was the Heinkel He 60. This aircraft was only chosen after trials with a number of others including the American Vought V85.

4 This view shows the forward torpedo tube position on the K-class cruisers. Four such sets were carried, port and starboard, forward and aft. Each set carried three tubes for the 50cm torpedo.

F: *EMDEN*

Emden, the first light cruiser to be built in Germany since the end of World War One, made a total of nine pre-war cruises as a cadet training ship, several of which saw her fully circumnavigate the globe. These 'flag-waving' cruises were a great success and did much to enhance the international image of Germany and her navy. Several of Germany's greatest naval figures, including the future CinC U-Boats and CinC Navy Karl Dönitz, took their turn as commander of this small cruiser during her pre-war heyday. Although not particularly powerful by the standards of those cruisers that followed her, she was a fine-looking ship. As well as her own heraldic crest, *Emden* carries a large Iron Cross motif on her bow, tribute to her predecessor, lost at the battle of the Falkland Islands in 1914.

Though relatively small compared with other warships, this view, showing her in port circa 1929, gives a realistic impression of her size in comparison with vehicles and figures on the dockside. After completing eight world cruises, an intended cruise to America in 1938 was cancelled as Germany's standing in the world community deteriorated due to the political situation at home. Her subsequent (ninth) cruise instead took her Bulgaria and Turkey. It was

to be her last peacetime mission before war erupted in Europe once again.

G: COLOUR SCHEMES

1 *Emden* is shown here circa spring–summer of 1941 wearing the scheme introduced for vessels serving in the Baltic. Mid-grey, with broad black and white bands running at angles across her hull and upperworks, it also featured darker areas at bow and stern and a false bow wave to give the impression of a shorter vessel, and was widely worn by all medium and large warships (including the *Bismarck*) at this time.

2 This view shows the *Emden* wearing a camouflage scheme used by her in Baltic waters during 1942. Her pale grey upper surfaces have been overpainted in a darker grey, all but for a small area of hull side at bow and stern. The effect is to give an impression of shorter length and the extremely sharp 'rake' of the forward edge of the darker is intended to deceive an observer into confusing her with a destroyer.

3 This view shows *Köln* in her 1943 camouflage scheme. Her pale grey upperworks have had a darker grey splinter disruptive scheme added. This scheme was typical of that used on many medium and larger warships during this period.

4 Here we see *Nürnberg* in a rather more elaborate scheme than normal. In addition to her pale grey basic scheme, she carries a two-tone grey splinter pattern, with white false bow wave. This scheme was worn during her operations from Norway in 1943.

This stern view of *Köln* shows the large bronze eagle emblem carried prior to the outbreak of war. It also shows to good effect the off-centre layout of turrets 'Bruno' and 'Caesar'.

INDEX